A Journey Through Grace

A Journey Through Grace

Becoming Sarah

ISBN-13:

978-1723473951

ISBN-10:

1723473952

Contents

ACKNOWLEDGMENTS

Though this book is about me, Melissa, it wouldn't be possible without those who have helped me along the way. I want to thank my family for their love and support.

My mom was so proud of this journey I was on. I'm so thankful I got to share part of it with her before God called her home. I still have a wonderful dad and a lot of family cheering me on in her place. My husband David, and my daughter Amber, are a constant source of support. They've seen me at my best, and worst, but love me anyway. I love you two more than you know.

I also want to thank my church family at Bell Chapel Assembly of God. You all are irreplaceable! I owe a lot of gratitude to my pastor, Chad Duvall, and my associate pastor, Christi Johnston. As you read on you will understand what an important role these two plays in my life. I was blessed with the best pastoral team!

My pastor's beautiful wife Belinda took time out of her busy life to edit the book for me. Without her help, you would agree with me that I am unqualified to write a book, but with God's help, here it is. I also want to express gratitude to my close friends, who are always by my side. I love you all, and I'm blessed to have you in my life.

From the bottom of my heart, I thank you all!

-Melissa-

FOREWARD

I am the pastor mentioned several times throughout this book. I want to say that it has been an amazing adventure watching Melissa in the natural, becoming Sarah in the supernatural. Although the process has been fraught with up and downs, they have all been part of the process of spiritual transformation. I am so very proud of Melissa for setting out to write this book. The openness and honesty she exhibits in the pages is just further proof of her becoming this new creature in Christ Jesus. As you read this book, my hope for and prayer is that you too will find the path of mercy and grace to become a transformed new creature in Jesus!

-Chad Duvall
Senior Pastor
Ada's Bells Chapel Assembly of God
Atkins, AR

Over the past 15 or so years, I have watched the word GRACE come alive in Melissa Brown. Through the good, through the hard, and through the lonely places of life, she has kept her footing in Christ. She is a servant with great wisdom and value. I smile as I watch her story unfold. You will truly be blessed reading her journey, and I'm sure you will see this Grace I have spoken of come alive to you too!

-Christi Johnston
Associate Pastor
Ada's Bells Chapel Assembly of God
Atkins, AR

PREFACE

2 Corinthians 12:8-9
Three times I pleaded with the Lord to take it away from me. But he said to me, "my grace is sufficient for you, for my power is made perfect in weakness."
Therefore, I will boast all the more gladly about my weaknesses, so that Christ's power May rest on me.

This passage sums my book up beautifully. I am weak and full of imperfections. Through my weakness, God's power is demonstrated and through the fire, I am refined!

Praise God!

-Melissa Brown
Author
Russellville, AR

The Conflict

My name is Melissa. I'm just like you. I've been broken, knocked down, and beat up more times than I can recall, and most often by my own two hands. I have failed. In fact, I failed often. My mind is a jungle of chaos, confusion and doubt that desperately need pruning. My thoughts defeat me. The biggest battle I have ever faced was the battle in my head. I'm full of self; self-pity, self-loathing, and self-hatred. I have the heart of a rebel convincing me that I desire to do bad things. I secretly sabotage every good thing that comes my way because I know myself better than anyone else knows me, or so I think. You see, God knows me more intimately than I even know myself. He knows my thoughts before I do.

Psalm 139
139 LORD**, you have examined me
   and know all about me.**
**²You know when I sit down and
when I get up.**
   **You know my thoughts before I
think them.**
**³You know where I go and where I
lie down.**
   You know everything I do.
⁴LORD**, even before I say a word,
   you already know it.**
**⁵You are all around me—in front
and in back—**
   and have put your hand on me.
**⁶Your knowledge is amazing to
me;**
   it is more than I can understand.

When I reflect on myself, I see this mean, controlling, yet out of control creature that no one should love, yet God loves me anyway. God loves me by choice, and He loves me on purpose. God sees all the beautiful things He planted inside of me. He sees potential in me. He sees a beautiful, God fearing woman in the making. God knows that I am a diamond in the rough. He sees my value, yet that has no bearing on His love for me. God loves me just as I am, not for who I will be someday.

God loves me so much that He called me by name, twice in fact. The first time He called me into existence, into my mother's womb. He knitted me, fashioned me, and equipped me with everything I needed to fulfill my destiny. God took every detail of my life into consideration. He foresaw every hardship and battle I would face and preprogrammed me with just the right amount of strength and endurance to finish strong, but not so strong that I wouldn't learn to lean on him in the process. God looked at His creation and upon reviewing every spec, He said, "It is very good."

For a span of time, God left me in the care of people that He trusted such as my parents, teachers, and a few different Pastors. He knew they would impart goodness into my life and would nurture the seeds that were placed within me. That went well for a while until I decided that I could take over. I was a big girl, mature, and could self-prune from here on out. I was WRONG! I didn't realize then how important it was to have such strong Godly counsel in my life. I allowed tares to be planted among the wheat and I cultivated and harvested all the wrong thoughts. Before long, everything spiraled out of control and it was beyond anything that I could repair on my own.

The God in Heaven, that sits on the throne of all creation, had every right to throw me over to the tormentor. Surely, I should have faced the utter wrath of God, yet, for reasons that go far deeper than my understanding, God loved me. He genuinely loved me!

God saw fit to call me by name again, only this time I heard Him with my spirit.

"Sarah" He said.

"Yes Lord?"

"I'm calling you deeper. I'm calling you into purpose. This journey will be the scariest and most rewarding journey you will ever walk. You will have a season of pure delight so that you can taste, know that I am good and that My plans for you are good. Then, you will go through a testing. This will be hard, but I promise to be with you every step. It will feel as though you are being buried beneath every burden you can possibly carry but fear not. This is only a planting phase so that I can grow your faith."

Imagine yourself in my shoes. God formed me, He knows my name is Melissa. His voice was so clearly speaking to me when He called me Sarah. Was God confused? Did He make a mistake? No! My bible tells me God is perfection and Satan is the author of confusion, not Abba! So, who is Sarah? Sarah is my anointing. Sarah is my strength. Sarah is God's will coming to life in a very faulty vessel. Sarah is all of Melissa's imperfections lining up to demonstrate God's Grace. Sarah is the seed that God planted in the very beginning. When I see scared, inadequate, broken, confused, rebellious, tainted, and unworthy- God sees Sarah. God has always seen Sarah and will always see Sarah, but still, He unconditionally loves Melissa.

Somewhere, deep inside, I have always known God's love for me. Sometimes I get lazy in the self-pruning and the weeds of life over take my mind. I lose that focus. This time I've gone too far. Not so far that God's love for me no longer exists. Nothing will ever truly separate me from the love of God.

Romans 8:37-39
No, in all these things we are more than conquerors through him who loved us. For I am sure that neither death nor life, nor angels nor rulers, nor things present nor things to come, nor powers, nor height nor depth, nor anything else in all creation, will be able to separate us from the love of God in Christ Jesus our Lord.

Then the testing begins! This time I have wandered further than my feelers can reach. I can't feel God's embrace. I can't feel God's conviction. It's a scary place. My mind rages with thoughts that I can't seem to submit. I have a fear that Sarah is missing forever. I deprived her of her needs. I kept my flesh fed while my spirit starved and Sarah left. Will she ever come back? Will God leave me too? Has He already left? Is that why I can't see him, can't hear Him, can't feel him?

My thoughts...this mind.... I can't stop it! This is too intense. I can't take it! I can't take one more second! I began to cry out, "God, this has to stop. Can you hear me at all? Do you still love me? God, I'm begging...no more silent treatment. Where are you? Where's Sarah? I'm Scared! Please Help! God? Are you listening? I'm sorry God. I really am sorry. I surrender. God, I submit!"

SLAM! A door slammed in my mind and everything went silent. The voices that were so cleverly disguised as my own immediately hushed. On the door there was a sign, GRACE! Grace slammed the door on insecurity, doubt, fear, rebellion, double mindedness, and so much more. The answer to my failure was GRACE. The answer to my weakness was GRACE. The answer to how the God that is so perfect and Holy could possibly love me is GRACE.

I understand now. I understand that no matter how much I mess up that God's grace will prevail, giving me love that I don't deserve, and His mercy will keep me from the harsh judgment that I do deserve. I get it now God. Thank you for loving me beyond any measure that I can ever describe.

"You're welcome Sarah. Welcome home. You passed the test."

Grace wins every time! I would like to take a few steps backward and share my story with you. I believe as you read it you will understand that though we are all very different we are also all very much the same.

The Beginning

I'm 37 years old. I've been married for almost 18 years and we have one daughter who is 16 years old. We are your typical family. Thanks to God's provision in our life, my husband was able to work and provide while I stayed home to raise and educate our daughter.

I grew up in a middle-class home with both parents and an older sister. Life was good. We went to a small, country, Assembly of God church. Though we were Pentecostal by name, I honestly don't remember seeing much Holy Ghost happening. For an A/G church it had a very calm atmosphere. I never want to dismiss my roots as unimportant. There was a foundation being laid in my life from the very beginning.

As a child, I had a major misconception of who God was. I knew God was a spirit and I knew of Heaven and Hell. I thought God was watching, trying to catch me being naughty so He could send me straight to Hell.

In my mind, God was this supreme, all knowing being that carefully chose only the most elite, perfect people and I just knew there was little chance of me making that cut. I have always been guilty of not believing in myself. I have a low confidence in myself that constantly tells me I will never be enough or do enough. I'm undeserving! I bet, it is safe to say, you have dealt with that voice too. However, as a little girl, I longed for the things of God. Eventually my family quit going to church, everyone but me.

I didn't really know what a relationship with God was, but I loved to be in His house. My love for church continued, but I always feared God. I didn't know how to love a God that I really didn't know...and I REALLY did not know how to let Him love me.

Around the age of 14, I discovered a "love" for the world. I began to test the waters of sin. It was fun for the moment, so little by little I took another step further. My first adventure in sin (intended sin) was alcohol. This may not make sense really, but my first drinking experience was forced. I'm sure if I had a backbone I could have maneuvered out of the situation, but I was being blackmailed and thought there was no way out.

 At first, I was furious. I considered myself a Christian, and now I was defiled. But at the same time, it fed a part of me that had never tasted before. It fueled a desire in me. The "mad" part of me decided then that I needed to be in control. I had been teased and bullied a little in school. I also mentioned I had an older sister, of course she liked to put me through the ringer. At this point in life I let people walk all over me, bash me, and trash me. It didn't matter. No more. Something stood up inside me, something ugly. The bullied became the bully.

The other part of me, the part that was awakened by the lure of the alcohol, was hooked. I liked the way it made me feel and the way it helped me relax and let loose. I liked the way it made me feel so grown up. Sadly, I let the alcohol set up roots in my life, and for the next several years, I had myself a new pet; a drinking problem. I am not going to spend a lot of time glorifying my sinful years, but I spiraled out of control. Sex, drugs, rebellion, bullying, lying, and much more dominated me until I was 19.

At the age of 19, I met the man who later would become my husband. Just a few days shy of my 20th birthday, I found out I was expecting. I was told early on in life that I would probably never have children due to some health issues, so I never really planned to have or to not have kids. I thought that decision was unfairly made for me.

As a child, when I was asked what I wanted to be when I grew up, my answer always remained the same. I never remember this answer wavering. "I want to be a mom, a really good one." Being a mom has always been my heart's desire. I really wanted three kids, but now I'm thankful God saw fit to only give me one. The statement above "gut punched" me. Here I am with this life growing inside of me. I have choices to make now because good moms do not do the things that I was doing.

Once again, I try this whole God thing. My boyfriend and I decided to marry and do this right. This world is stinking hard, and if we were going to be good parents, then we knew we had to do it together. February 17th, 2001, we pledged to stick beside one another, no matter where this road led...better or worse right? Then on August 23, 2001, I laid eyes on the most beautiful creature I have ever seen in my entire life. It was that moment, that I first held my daughter, I realized I never knew what love was before.

I had never felt that feeling towards my husband or God. I realized I didn't know God, I didn't love God, I simply had a form of religion but absolutely no relationship. As you can guess, this God thing didn't last. Before long both myself and my husband spiraled back out of control.

The Real Beginning

In 2003, my husband had a good job working for a Christian man whose #1 ministry was soul winning. He relentlessly invited my husband to church. My husband was ready, but I was not. I was very much caught up in sin and still very much loving it. We learn in Hebrews 11:25 there is pleasure in sin for a season. Little did I know; my season was coming to a halt.

That man prayed for us and pure misery set in. One day, he invited us to a singing. I agreed to go if he would get off my back. He agreed. I went thinking, "I like gospel music. No harm." That day, God totally wrecked me! The Holy Ghost was MOVING! I had never witnessed anything like it before. I was scared; terrified actually. My heart was pounding. I could feel something I had never felt before ... CONVICTION! I fought the pull so hard, but, when I left there I was filled with the Holy Ghost with evidence of speaking in other tongues and I was water baptized.

I cannot explain how free I felt. It was such a liberating experience! For the next week I felt so full of the Holy Ghost I could barely eat. My flesh was fine, but my spirit was craving more.

Instantly I was delivered from all the sins that are often hard to kick. I was freed from addiction. Praise God! We continued to go to this church for approximately 8 years. I was growing and moving up in ministry, which is a place I never saw myself. I was involved in bus ministry, fund raising, and teaching. I enjoyed it. I wish that could be my happy ending, but I fell into a "works" mentality. I was busy doing great things for the Lord but got lazy in my relationship. I let offense creep in and knock me down. We explained to our Pastor that we felt our time there had ended, and God was moving us on. The truth- I ran from my calling and anointing.

I think, as you read on, you will notice the pattern, so I will just throw myself under the bus…I'm notorious for tucking tail and taking off. Yep, I'm a runner.

It took us a year before we landed in another church that felt right for us. We were looking, but nothing seemed right. I had good intentions. My feelings were hurt so I was going to find a new church and get a fresh start. However, no one fought for me. They wished me luck and let me go. Nobody asked us to stay. Nobody asked us what was wrong or offered to help. I know it was obvious we were running away from an issue, and nobody really bought into the lie I had fed them. I faced a familiar enemy- rejection. That overwhelming feeling of not being loved set in quickly. In that year span of being in between churches, I spiraled back downhill. I 100% turned my back on God, but I'm so thankful that He never once turned His back on me.

We found a church in a little bitty town about forty minutes from where we live. The town population was in the 600's yet the church consistently ran in the 200's. We loved everything about the church. We pushed in and rededicated ourselves back to God. We stayed at this church for about 4 years. I desired to help, to be a worker in the church, but the church already had adequate help. There seemed to be no place for me to serve. I grew unhappy with that, and I took it to God in prayer. I thought God would open a place for me to serve in the church- IN THAT CHURCH. God had other plans.

If you need to know more about the Holy Ghost, or Holy Spirit as some say, then I want to suggest a sermon that my Pastor has preached that might help you. At the end of the book I will explain how you can view this sermon as well as others.

- **Holy Ghost**

About Face- A Call to Repentance

One day when I was in prayer, God laid a church on my mind. I had been there once when a lady friend of mine was ministering, and her husband's band led worship. Though I had attended once, I knew nothing about this church. It had been a long time since I had been there. I asked God to clarify what He was showing me. Soon I realized God was calling me there to be a part of that congregation.

Something else you need to know about me, I hate change! Change is scary. If it is my idea then I will take a chance, but I do not like being forced. Good news is God will never force anyone to do anything or go anywhere. God grants us freewill, and I was determined to exercise mine, "No thank you God.   I'm comfortable here." I was content and moving again was not on my agenda. Little did I know; my spirit had also grown content. I was in a place where I was no longer growing.

I began to pray some more. I confided in two friends. I and asked them to help me pray for God's will and peace to accept it. One day I went to my home church. I felt great, but when I got there I instantly got sick, very sick. I had no choice but to go home. Service hadn't even started yet. Before I could get home, I felt fine, very fine. It was crazy. I went home and laid down anyway. I started thinking that God probably had something up His sleeve.

A few hours later my phone rang. It was my friend from church, the same friend that had ministered a few years back at the church that I was feeling called to. She had called to check on me since it was abnormal for me to just leave with no warning. She proceeded to tell me her good/bad news. "I wanted to let you know I made an announcement today that I would be leaving the church in a few months. God has blessed me with an opportunity. I have been asked to be the Associate Pastor at another church." This friend was not one of my two friends that I had confided in, so image my reaction when she told me the name of the church. You guessed it. It was the very church that God was leading me to. Coincidence? Not a chance! That was the moment I knew that God was in fact calling me to that church. I didn't know why, but I accepted it, as did my family. We went, and we loved it!

My current church was a beautiful building inside and out. I was a bit disappointed in the physical physique of the new church. Small plain building, ugly carpet, hard pews…it's just a good thing I don't judge a book by its cover. Inside that little church I found a true treasure. Never have I felt more love. Not once have I felt the Holy Spirit in such a strong capacity. Never have I heard such profound wisdom flow from the pulpit. On no occasion have I experienced God the way I have in this church. This church is called Ada's Bells Chapel Assembly of God (Bells Chapel) in Atkins AR. (The church has been remodeled and added to since. It's beautiful.)

When God led me to this church it was the best thing for my relationship with Him. The moment I submitted to this change, a lot of things were set into motion. This is where my story really begins.

The Butterfly Emerges

Somewhere through the years I went from this full of life, loud mouthed kid, to a very shy, guarded person. I was very careful to hide amongst the crowd and go unnoticed. At Bells Chapel that was hard to do. Everyone wanted to know my story. Everyone wanted to be my friend. Honestly at this point I didn't know how to maintain a healthy friendship. Most of my friendships were one sided. I could be your friend. I could listen and help and do everything a friend should do, but that's it. I couldn't let anyone be or do those things for me. Life was lonely- but here I was once again with a fresh start laid before me.

My husband never meets a stranger and we were being invited to hang out with people from church. I wasn't sure if it was a good idea, but I did it; I allowed myself to have friends. It was nice, and before very much time passed, these friends became family. Sure, sometimes they drive me batty, I'm human, but I wouldn't trade a single one of them. I adore my church family. This church is truly different, and I've never experienced anything remotely close. My soul was being fed in a deeper manner. I had been on the milk of God's word for so long, but I finally got a meat experience. I tasted, and I liked it.

A hunger rose up in me and I literally craved God's word. It was here I learned the importance of self-feeding. I had never spent much time in prayer or digging into God's word for myself. My idea of God time at home was pulling up my favorite worship songs on YouTube and bellowing them out to the top of my lungs while I was doing my house hold chores. That was no longer going to satisfy the longing in my spirit. I was hooked, and God became the desire of my heart.

Something strange yet completely normal happened. The closer I got to God, the more I began to realize how human I was. In His presence I began to feel very unworthy and "less than". I stated that it was normal because I think at some point we all fight the demon of self-worth but that is not something God puts on us. Remember in Chapter 1 I told you I had a Holy Ghost encounter? What I failed to mention was that I had an extremely difficult time allowing myself to completely surrender, so that experience didn't happen very often. I wasn't one of those people who could just open my mouth and let my heavenly prayer language flow. I was notorious for quenching the spirit. It eventually became such a problem that my heart became hardened.

I redeveloped a hunger for the spirit of God and began to seek a refilling. What I didn't realize until later was, when I closed myself off to the world, I actually closed myself off to God. I was still saved and living right, but I was so guarded that God couldn't move in my heart. It's easy to find ourselves in this position. My pastor calls it a brass heaven.

Deuteronomy 28:23
And thy heaven that *is* over thy head shall be brass, and the earth that *is* under thee *shall be* iron.

It feels as though heaven is completely shut away from you and as though God doesn't hear your prayers. As a matter of fact, sometimes it feels as though your prayers hit the ceiling and fall right back down, punching you in the gut.

It is so easy to blame Satan for the brass heaven syndrome. *Satan blocked my prayer. Satan stopped my blessing. Satan robbed my joy....* or worse, sometimes we even blame God. *If God would only listen. If God would only respond. If God would only change this or do that then things would be okay.* The reality is, sometimes I am to blame. ME! My thoughts, my actions, my reactions can and will place a wedge between me and my Father. That wedge is driven out through repentance, but it is hard to repent when you don't know what you are doing wrong or even realize that you are making a mistake.

I didn't realize my heart had become so calloused. At this moment in life, things were going well. I felt as if God had "brick walled" me, and I didn't understand why! He didn't! Unaware, I "brick-walled" my savior. It was through prayer, fasting, Pastoral counseling, and self-reflection that the answer finally came. I want to pause here and share an actual entry from my journal.

On 1-15-17 I wrote:

I recently went through a very intense counseling session with my Pastor and his team. I didn't understand the process. Also, I was embarrassed and ashamed that I needed to be there. I know during the process that I did not yield to Father. The next day I seemed worse. I was more bitter, angrier, and more anxious. I was mad enough that I cried out to God asking a lot of "why's". God clearly answered. I had concentrated so hard on sealing myself off to everyone and everything that unfortunately I had sealed God out too.   I had a barrier, and no one could cross it. In my mind I was strong, and I didn't need anyone. Since I refused to believe I was weak, God couldn't move. In my weakness He is strong- Not in my stubbornness! My counseling session was not in vain. It opened my eyes to things I needed to call out, confess, forsake, and get over. God opened my eyes to GRACE. God loves me despite my imperfections; in the same manner that I love my daughter. He uses my imperfections to speak into others. The next few days my prayers were different. Then Sunday morning, I had my shift. I was worshipping at the front of the church. My Pastor made a call that if you needed a specific healing to come to the center. I did. I stood directly in front of the platform. My heart was ready because of everything that had taken place that week. I had a hunger for God and grace on my side. I began praying, asking God to heal my back, but I felt God nudge me saying that I needed a healing far greater than that. I began crying out to God. I'm telling you my deliverance was very much a process. I'm still going through the transformation, but my broken spirit was mended.

That day, the brass heaven and brick wall were shattered! That day a veil was torn between me and Abba and I was refilled with his spirit. I wish I could say I hadn't struggled since then to press into God's presence but the more I "practice" His presence, the better I get at submitting to the Holy Spirit.

If this is an area of struggle for you then I want to suggest a few sermons that my Pastor has preached that might help you

- **Brass Heaven**
- **Shattering the Brass Heaven through Prayer and Fasting**
- **The Man in the Middle**

Grace Revealed and Growth Instilled

As hard as this is for me, the Holy Spirit is prompting me to be real and raw. I'm simply going to share a few inserts from my journal, so you can see my journey for yourself.

1-18-17

So many things have been taking place deep within me. There are things I can't begin to describe because I'm not sure I understand the fullness of everything. What I do know is I have experienced a shift and I like it. Over the years I have unknowingly allowed bad seeds to be planted in my mind. There were seeds of anger, doubt, fear, distrust, resentment, and so much more. These seeds took root. Looking back, I realized that I am guilty of feeding and nurturing them. My soul has been thorny for a long time, but God is calling me out. God is speaking life where there was no life. God is purging me of darkness, lies, rage, and self-torment and is opening my eyes up to see GRACE.

GRACE IS A BEAUTIFUL THING!

1-27-17

**Psalm 119:71
It is good for me that I have been afflicted so that I may learn your statutes.**

Statutes by biblical definition is a law or decree made by a sovereign God.

To me, this is God's judgement, God's peace, God's plan, and God's promises; everything God has spoken to us and over us. In an essence, it is who or what God is to us.

So, I read, it is good that I am afflicted or tested so I can truly understand what my God is made of. How can I have a favorite actor if I never saw him act or a favorite wrestler if I never saw him wrestle? The same holds true with God. How can He be my peace maker if I never had conflict? How can God be my deliverer if I never had bondage? How can he be my healer if I was never sick? How can He be my chain breaker if I never had chains? God allows me to go through every trial, every hardship, every ounce of affliction for a greater purpose; for His purpose. It is not to bring me down, but it is to raise God up because when I am weak, He is strong!

1-29-17

I hear so often (and even feel this way myself sometimes) that I am so flawed and can never measure up to the most Holy God. That isn't so much of an issue now that I am understanding GRACE! However, it was nice to open my bible and be reminded that God purposely chooses the flawed and imperfect. If God put a light inside of a vase and put a lid on it, then the light wouldn't be seen. It wouldn't serve a purpose. However, if the vase had cracks you would be able to see the light pierce through the cracks. I am nothing more than a cracked pot! I have broken pieces and in much need of repair, but God has placed His light within me. As His light pierces through all my shortcomings, it makes a difference to a very dark world. I'm so thankful that God uses my brokenness and my flaws for His glory.

2-6-17

I was reading 1 Chronicles 29. Mostly this chapter is the details of building the temple and I didn't get anything from most of this passage, but God's word doesn't return void, right? Verse 1 stuck out at me. Solomon who is now known for his wisdom was being appointed as the next king. God had chosen him even though he was young and inexperienced. That is how I feel, young and inexperienced, yet God chose me. He chose ME! I didn't choose God, I ran from Him, but He called me by name. He set me apart from the world and placed a light within me! God knew when He called me, I wasn't equipped for the job, and He doesn't need me to remind him every day. As I walk through each day in obedience, He will give me what I need to complete each task at hand. I just must be willing to be willing!

I have shared my journal entries to demonstrate that the more I grew, the more I understood grace. The more I understand grace, the more I continue to grow. This process should never end. There will always be a deeper revelation, and a new level in Christ Jesus always awaits us.

If understanding grace is a struggle for you then please check out these sermons from my Pastor:

- **Theo Pistis (God Faith)**
- **Access**
- **Legacy series**

The Birth of Sarah

On Sunday, March 5th, 2017, I was at my church and the spirit was really flowing. As mentioned, I was going through a lot of changes. God was beginning to come to life in me. There is a man in my church who is very dear to me. He has traveled all over the world evangelizing, but this day God sent him to me. He took me by both hands and said, "Melissa, God has taken you from negative to positive but now He is trying to take you from positive to prophetic. You have to yield to Him." I blushed and said, "Thank you." I could totally see that I wasn't such a negative person anymore.

Before, if someone cut me off, messed up my order, or talked down to me, it would be plastered on my social media, but I cleaned that up. My thoughts conformed to Philippians 4:8 and I began thinking on things that are true, honest, just, pure, lovely, and of good report and I began to post and speak blessings and declarations over the people I love and even myself, but the thought of moving from positive to prophetic was intimidating. A good side note is God never intimidates us.

Intimidation is a form of control which stems from the spirit of witchcraft. God gives us freewill. He offered this gift to me and I had the power to choose. It was Satan that manipulated my thoughts to think that I am not worthy of such a gift and for a moment, I bowed to that. I laughed within myself and said to God, "Who me? Prophetic? Used for your Glory? I think he (the evangelist) got the wrong girl." I completely dismissed the thoughts.

On Wednesday, March 8th, I had one of the craziest God experiences I have ever had. I was in prayer meeting at my church. There was just a hand full of people there. We all find our own private place to pray for an hour while music plays in the background. At the end, we circle up and pray corporately. Prayer meeting had been dismissed and I was gathering my things to leave. My Pastor stopped me and said he had a word from the Lord to give me. This always makes me nervous. The following is my journal entry recalling this experience.

3-8-17

Wow! God is good! This morning I was at prayer meeting at Bells Chapel. I was sitting in my normal place and was just praying over the needs written on the board. A song came on and the lady was singing, "change my name, I no longer feel the same. I won't let go until you bless my soul, just change my name." It caught my attention and I paused and said, "God change my name. I'm not even sure what I mean but change my name. I don't feel like myself anymore." Then I simply went back to my regular praying. After prayer meeting, Pastor came to me and said, "I have a word for you. The Lord said your new name will be Sarah. Just as Sarah heard the voice of the Lord and laughed behind the tent door, so have you heard a promise and laughed within yourself, questioning, is it really possible? Could this happen to me? So, from this day forward, the Lord will call you Sarah. God says to prepare yourself to receive the promise in due time just like Sarah did when she gave birth to Isaac." Wow, I'm blown away! I'm not even sure why I paused to say "change my name" but, wow! I'm not sure what all this means but I will chase it and I will find it.

It wasn't until later I realized, the word I received from Pastor corresponded to the word I have received on the previous Sunday. I had a spoken promise from God, but I stood behind the door of my heart and laughed in disbelief. I repented, and I began to chase God harder.

The following Sunday, I had journaled about another experience. A lady came to pray with me. To my knowledge she never touched me, but she stood in front of me fanning, as if to fan a flame. The Holy Spirit overwhelmed me. It felt as though large gusts of wind were blowing me backwards as I prayed in tongues. I could feel an anointing stirring in my belly.

The next day, March 13th, I was reflecting on my week. I had grown so much and was in complete awe of what God was doing. However, I was still struggling with the battle in my head that consistently and relentlessly questions my worth. I really struggled allowing myself to surrender. I was no longer a commoner standing in the outer courts, I had made my way into the inner courts, but I had a yearning to go all the way into the Holy of Holies. I knew that God had opened that up to me the very moment that He took my place at Calvary, but the struggle was real.

That day I text my Pastor and asked for advice. "How do I get past my own head so that I can fully yield?" His answer spoke volumes to me. He wrote," *Seek and ye shall find...knock and it shall be opened to you! He is a pearl of great price, worth all the effort, all the frustration, all the questioning…yes, He is worth it all! Do not get weary in the seeking. Grow only stronger, knowing that today may just be the day that the veil opens to you and you get to see Him and know Him."*

After that, God revealed to me that I had been chasing Him but not seeking Him.

<u>Chase</u>- pursue in order to catch or to make contact with someone to get something owed or required

<u>Seek</u>- attempt to find or desire to obtain or achieve

The difference between "chase" and "seek" can be such a fine line but can leave such a large void in our lives. The chase and the seek are both important and I'm learning it is a lifelong process. Day by day, God was and is revealing things to me.

On 3-13-17 I penned these words:

I feel like a geode. I have a rough, ugly, unattractive exterior. No one sees what is hidden inside. When you open a geode, it is lined with beautiful crystals that you cannot see until the rock has been broken. Just like a geode, God has hidden beautiful things inside of me. I'm just learning to access it and as I allow myself to become broken for His glory, then the beauty that is within me will be revealed. There is much beauty to be found in my brokenness!

3-14-17 (partial entry)

I started praying, "God, how do I make my prayers more meaningful and powerful, not just empty words? I know you hear me, answer me, and care when I pray but how do I go deeper in prayer? How do I move mountains?" Suddenly, tongues were activated, and I was bawling my eyes out. The spirit is subject to the flesh and I could turn it off but whenever I would stop praying in tongues I could feel it welling up inside like a fountain; like a geyser that was about to blow full force. At one point I said, "I don't know what I am praying but I trust that this is how mountains are moved." At this point pictures of people started running through my head like film running through a projector. I had been lying in bed thinking of my life and all this newness coming to me. I hadn't been thinking of anyone or anything else. Perhaps I tapped into my father's heart.

I later realized that part of being Sarah was a call to intercession. I could write pages upon pages, revealing my journal to you but I will leave some things between me and the Lord. I will tell you that I dove deeper and deeper into God's love. I began writing songs effortlessly- they just come to me when I am in prayer or worship and I mostly keep them private and sing them back to God during our intimate time. I also had my first experience at delivering a message in tongues. (gift of tongues 1 Corinthians 12:8-11) I was loving

growing and learning as the Holy
Spirit led me.

Speed of Battle

In April 2017, God began to lay something on my heart. I didn't know why I needed to do this, but I followed the spirit. I went to my parent's church on a Monday and joined them for their weekly prayer meeting. God had me kneel at my parent's seat and travail in intercession for them. I didn't know what I was praying, nor did I know the battle that was just ahead. This was not a one-time thing. I went every Monday night for a few months. I could only see to the corner, but God could see around the corner. He knew that both myself and my parents needed that extra prayer.

The following Wednesday (4-19-17), I was in a prayer meeting at my church. I was sitting still with my head resting on the seat in front of me and suddenly I became very dizzy. I thought something was wrong, but immediately God dropped this into my spirit. He said, "I just notched up the Potter's wheel. Hold on." Wow!

God was doing amazing, incredible things inside of me but that was an issue; all the changes were internal. At this point God began to give me dreams and visions. Though I have each one documented, I don't feel that they are a part of this story. I was yielding to the spirit and "becoming Sarah", but I still went home to the life that Melissa had made over the last 36 years. At the end of April something significant happened.

The more I "became Sarah", the more I realized how imperfect my (Melissa's) life really was. I remember texting my Pastor for his advice. My question was this, "I'm tired. If I just divorce my husband and move on where that puts me with my ministry?" My husband is a good man and so I don't want anyone drawing conclusions or filling in the blanks. We had been stagnant for a while and things between us were cold. I knew God only allowed divorce for certain reasons, we did not fall under those guidelines. I had convinced myself that I could just divorce him and repent later, but I liked my place in the church. I loved the growth I was experiencing, and I didn't want any of that to change.

Pastor answered me just like he often does- with homework. He challenged me to spend the next five days in prayer on behalf of my marriage. Each day I had a question I was to present to God and I was instructed to allow God to respond. I took this very seriously. I sat aside time to talk to God each day. I only discussed the issue at hand during this time. I wrote down my prayer for each day, then I wrote God's response.

 Many people think that God doesn't speak but if you listen, He does. I prayed, God spoke!

He said, *"I called you Sarah, not Hagar. Are you going to birth an Ishmael in your life through impatience or will you trust me and wait for your promised Isaac?"*

Has my marriage been miraculously healed? No, there is work to do, but I have a promise to wait on; so, I set aside the thoughts of divorce and began to pray for my marriage.

God really dealt with me about my thinking patterns and my impatience. Impatience is the seed of bad choices. Fast forward to May. The battle kicked into overdrive. Due to strong emotions that this will bring up, I will again just copy my journal entry for the day.

5-15-17

I have heard sermon after sermon about when tragedy strikes, about when you get THAT call, today was my day. Today I found out that my mom has stage 4 cancer. I tried to fight emotion. I tried to fight fear. As tears slowly rolled down both cheeks, we proceeded to ask questions of the doctor. I wish I could say his responses were hopeful, but they weren't. The doctor had no solid answers for my mom's future. He couldn't tell us how fast she would heal. He couldn't tell us how far it had spread. He couldn't tell is if treatments would help. All he could tell us was the current facts, which was that my mom had gallbladder cancer and it had at least spread to her liver. I don't have the answers. I don't know if chemo will make a difference, but I know prayer will. As soon as we left from talking to the doctor, I went to the restroom and I cried. A Lot! Hard! I text my Pastor and I told him the bad news and I ended my text like this, "How do I be a Sarah? What do I do?" Pastor said, "In a moment like this, all a Sarah can do is have faith in Abba and how much He loves us and just stand still." I started praying. "How much faith do I have? I know it only takes a small amount, but what if my faith is tainted by doubt or fear?" God answered, "It doesn't matter what measure of faith I have, His grace is sufficient!" I have a lot of thoughts racing through my mind, but at the end of the day, my thoughts or emotions don't matter. My words and my reactions count. That is where the power lies.

5-20-18

On 5-18, my parents set my family down and explained more about the cancer. The doctor told her it was terminal. My mind exploded into a thousand directions. Over the past several days, I've experienced a lot of emotions. I've thought a lot, and I've prayed a lot. One thing I have learned over the past several days is that emotions are not signs or dictators of my faith. My heartbreak that I feel is normal and will not dictate or weaken my faith. I was praying one day, and I was telling God that I was caught off guard. My mom was having a simple in and out surgery, which turned into a more complex surgery, which turned into bad news, which turned into unthinkable news. In my eyes, my whole world was just flipped upside down. Then God said, "What changed between today and yesterday?" He made me understand that today isn't any worse than yesterday because yesterday my mom had cancer too. Reality hadn't changed, my perspective had changed. I had perceived that in an overall manor, my mom was still healthy but unaware reality had changed some time ago. God had just allowed it to be brought to our attention for whatever reason. None of this caught God by surprise. He knew the moment the cancer contacted her body. He takes time to count every hair on her body. Hair is so insignificant. It has no purpose beyond fueling our vain beauty. If God will take time to count every hair, then how much more attentive will he be with the things in our body? I believe He knows every single cell.

5-23-18

I was singing:
Zion is calling me
To a higher place of praise
To stand upon a mountain
And magnify his name…
(I do not own rights to the song.)

God asked me to define my mountain. My current mountain is that the doctor is trying to stamp my mom with an expiration date. Cancer *is my mountain. God said, "stand on that mountain and magnify my name and I will usher you into higher praise!"*

From May to November, I continued to write about my God experiences, about our journey through cancer, and even though Melissa had a broken heart, Sarah was soaring. God revealed himself in so many ways. His hand was always evident in the situation. I didn't want to be in this battle, but I was learning and growing through the process. I thought my mom's healing would come through my obedience to God like it was just a test of my faith.   It was a test of faith but not in the sense that I thought. I jumped through every hoop that God set before me and I carefully guarded my mouth gate. Sarah was strong and did everything right without hesitation, so of course God was going to heal my mom. Why would He not?

I watched my mom's faith grow. She used to ask me questions about my faith. She didn't understand how a person could ever know for certain that they are saved. The bible says the gate is narrow and few will find it. This always made Mom question her own relationship with God. She was stuck in that phase of, *"Am I doing it right? Am I doing enough?"* Without going through the test of cancer, she may have never been able to answer her own questions with certainty, but one day she looked at me and said, "I'm ready! I know Heaven will be my home and I have the peace that I have been looking for."

We chased every avenue of healing; prayer, specialists, medicines, surgeries, anything we could find that might help. For a few months we received good reports but by the end of the year my mom's health was in complete failure. I watched my mom suffer, but I was amazed at her strength. She never complained, never gave up, and her faith never wavered. We got to spend one more Christmas together, followed by her 61st birthday in

January. Then, February 5th, God called my momma home.

As mentioned, my mom suffered immensely over the last few months. The very moment that she took her last breath on earth, you could see a look of peace upon her face. My mom's promised miracle was not a miracle of earthly healing, but it was the miracle of Heaven; an everlasting healing. It was a sad but beautiful moment. Her peace that she found in that instant, became a peace that I grabbed hold of for myself. I knew that I would need to remember that look of bliss, so I could get myself through the lonely moments that would lie just ahead.

I didn't realize until I was writing this book that God did not tell me to worship Him, and He would heal my mother. He told me to worship Him and He will take me into a higher praise. God was teaching me to praise Him through one of my darkest hours. I did. Somedays I was angry. I didn't understand why my mom had to go, but death is only for sinner's. My mom is alive and well, dancing on the streets of Heaven! I never blamed God. I praised Him for the good and I praised Him for the bad. I praised Him for what I understood and comprehended, and I praised Him for the unknown. I praised Him for every victory, and I even praised Him for the battle. Praise is our weapon in the warfare we fight, and this is one fight that I am going to win!

Go read the story of Jehoshaphat in 2 Chronicles, chapter 20. All odds were stacked against them, but by praise, they won the victory. When you're in a situation, and you don't know what else to do, just praise your way out.

The Battle Rages On

I had been on a weight loss journey that began around the same time as my mom's battle began. My mom was my biggest encourager. She wanted me to get healthy. Twenty-one days after my mom passed, I had a weight loss surgery called Duodenal Switch. I've done really well with the weight loss part of the surgery, but I've had a lot of complications that stemmed from the surgery.

A few days after surgery I found out I had gallstones. The stones were already there, but my new diet inflamed my gallbladder causing it to rear its ugly head. I have not had it removed at this time, but that is in my near future. I have had more than my fair share of ER visits for dehydration, and I am very deficient in several vitamins and minerals. Due to my lack of fluid intake, I also developed a kidney stone which had to be removed by emergency surgery after a month of trying to pass it.

Things could have been worse, but it hasn't been too bad, all things considered. I have no regrets. Weight loss surgery saved my life!

I have done fairly well with losing my mom. Life is certainly different. My mom was my best friend, and we did everything together. We would do crafts, play games, shop, and yard sale. We were next door neighbors, so our lives intertwined so much on a day to day basis. Also, when my mom passed, I tried to take on the role of caring for my dad. He didn't need anyone to care for him, but I tried anyway.

After surgery I dealt with a few weeks of pain. I've never really acknowledged this before, but when I took the pain pills it was like swallowing Satan's poison. I took them as prescribed. I've never had any type of pill addiction. I don't want it to sound like that or anything, it's just that I had went through two major life changes in less than a month, all while still borderline hating my husband that God would not allow me to leave. Now, add hydrocodone to the mix, along with pain, and a lot of downtime. Satan flooded me!

I began to really struggle with depression. I started questioning God with the "whys". I even accused God of making a fool out of me. I'm in ministry at my church though, and I wanted to uphold the standard that I knew my pastor and God expected from me, so I chose to fight this alone instead of reaching out. Everyone had such high expectations for "Sarah" and I don't like to disappoint.

I have two modes, perfection or nothing. If I don't feel like I can do something very well then, I don't want to do it at all. Who wants to be a failure? I kept pushing, but only hard enough to appear that I was okay. I was certainly not okay! God tried to send help my way. People would try to pray with me. I was given several words of knowledge, but I never really responded to any of it.

Then, as though I'm not already at the edge, I came really close to losing my daughter. She's sixteen and had asthma since birth.

Attacks come and land her in the emergency room on a regular basis. On a good day her lungs only function about 50%. She's too young to die and too young to be this ill. As a matter of fact, please pray for her, your prayer may be the prayer of faith that she needs. This day she was having an asthma attack and we were preparing to go to the hospital. I had stepped into the restroom while she was finishing her current breathing treatment. I was gone two minutes at the most.

When I returned, my daughter was collapsed in the floor, totally unresponsive. She wasn't breathing. She was blue and laying in a puddle of urine. I panicked. I thought I had found my daughter dead. This was hands down the scariest day of my life.

She collapsed with her head on an air mattress that we had set up for guests. The room was small, and we used it like storage, so I could barely get to her. I was so panicked. I called 911 but the whole time I was saying, "Help me God…. Amber breath!" I just said the same thing over and over while kicking the air bed, thinking it would wake her up.

I remember the operator saying, "Ma'am, is it just you and Amber in the house?" I said no, "It is me, Amber and God!" Amber starting slowly gasping for air on her own, I never had to start CPR. I know that God was with us and that He is the reason that Amber is still alive! Thank God we haven't had any more scares since then.

Then, I have a close friend who I've known over twenty years. She's more of a sister to me. We really have "been there, done that and got the t-shirt". We have a lot of stories we could tell; some good, some bad.

Though I'm sharing her story with permission, it's not really my story to tell, so I'm going to just get right to the important details. She was twenty-seven weeks pregnant with a baby girl when she suddenly developed double pneumonia. The pneumonia went septic and she developed ARDS. She was put in ICU at our local hospital. She was then med flighted to Baptist Hospital in Little Rock, Arkansas. The staff their saved her life!

The stress that her body was enduring was too much and her placenta ruptured. Her body was trying to abort the baby. The medical team responded quickly with an emergency c-section. It was successful, but both mom and baby came out of surgery on a ventilator. The baby was so tiny. She was less than 3 pounds, but, all things considered, we had a healthy baby girl.

Sometime during this ordeal, my friend had a stroke. It went undetected until she came to from a medically induced coma. The mom had a long road to recovery after a month in the hospital, and in some areas, she is still recovering but luckily this situation turned out okay. The baby is still in the hospital and weighs over eight pounds. She's healthy but can't come home until she can take a bottle more frequently.

My friend and her husband have an amazing story of their own that demonstrates God's grace. They had found themselves on the wrong path. We are all on the wrong path to start off with, we are born into sin. They were at the end of the path though. Drugs were destroying their family at a very rapid rate. They found themselves with no other place to turn except Jesus. Out of desperation, they called out to Him and He was faithful. God met them at that altar and extended that same grace to them as He did to me.

Can you imagine being in the shoes of this man? God had restored everything that Satan had attempted to destroy, but here he was on the brink of destruction again. This man watched his wife and newborn baby struggle for every breath they took. He did not know if either of them would live. Fear and lies set up in his mind. He should have run to God but in the middle of battle, we often go into fight or flight mode. He didn't have any fight left in him and he made the wrong choice. This was a relapse moment for him.

He isn't a bad guy, a bad husband, or a bad dad, but he did make some very bad decisions for himself which landed him in jail. When his wife awoke from her medically induced coma, all she wanted was her husband, but he wasn't available. Medical staff advised us to withhold this information for as long as possible because the last thing my friend needed was more stress.

I obliged, as we all did, but this was my "sister" and I was lying to her. It didn't feel right and I struggled with guilt because of it. I tried to mask my guilt by helping. I went to Little rock at least every other day and would spend the day trying to take care of my friend's needs. I'm not always innocent but in this situation, I honestly feel like I did everything the way Jesus would want me to, except lying about her husband's situation, even though it was for her health.

During all of this, there was some unnecessary drama that came up with her family. Though I had done nothing but help, all the drama was aimed at me. Nothing that I did was good enough for them. I either did too much or too little. They had no idea what they were doing to me, because they had no idea I was on the verge of a meltdown. In my eyes, they were outside sources who were looking in on the situation but were not trying to be a part of the solution. For a disclaimer, I am not talking about my friend's entire family. There were a few certain ones that were determined to make me miserable and they succeeded. I refuse to elaborate on the details. I have forgiven those who wronged me. It wouldn't be fair to exploit the situation any further.

I felt as though I was experiencing hell on earth over these past few months.

Where's Sarah?

I know it's not an excuse, but the battles I went through literally broke me. I cracked! I should have run to God and in many ways, I did, but I failed miserably.   I'm really embarrassed to write this chapter, but I refuse to live in condemnation. Every sin, every failure, is under the blood and I'm free!

For those who know me personally, please note that it is so uncomfortable to pour from my heart. There is a part of me that is embarrassed to write this chapter, but this is my story of Grace and this chapter is important. Real people have mess ups and disappointments. My goal is through my mistakes, you will see God's perfection.

It all started with my thoughts. *Sarah failed... God failed... Even Melissa failed. God was finished with me, He never heard my cries for help. He no longer cared.*

I became angry and bitter as I ate the lies of the enemy. Those people that I forgave in chapter 9, forgiveness did not come fast enough, and certainly not before I called them some nasty names, names that don't typically flow out of this mouth. I should have felt conviction of the Holy Spirit, but I didn't. I felt empowered! It felt good and releasing.

Remember, I'm in Ministry. I'm a faithful tithe payer. I love the Lord. I love my church and the last thing I want to do is be a hypocrite working in the church. There's no bigger turn off to the unsaved as a hypocrite. I did what I thought was right. I exposed my wrong-doings to my pastor. Here is a good place to tell you that I tried to quit my position in the church. I was not upholding the standard that was expected of me. I was not representing my church well, or even God for that matter. My pastor wouldn't allow me to. He said, "I'm not going to throw you away like a piece of trash, I still see your value." It was not because he was willing to "wink" at my sin or sweep it under the rug. He wasn't going to turn a blind eye to my errors. My pastor acknowledged that I was wrong. He basically assured me that I am human, and I would make mistakes. He told me I needed to repent, forsake, and move forward.

Pastor Chad knew that I needed to feel needed and if he would have dismissed me from my duties then there was nothing to keep me coming. During my battle, I felt obligated to come to church and fulfill the duties that were assigned to me. Pastor knew I would not let him down.

I should have felt honored that he was so understanding and so forgiving. I really should have taken his advice, but I didn't. I fueled my anger. I kept using those words. I turned on myself. I was improving my health at this point in my weight loss journey. I was down almost 100 lb. I should have been proud, but the more weight I lost, the uglier I felt. I had never been one to put down my body. I knew I was extremely overweight. It wasn't healthy, but I loved who I was as a human being, at least most of the time. Suddenly, I begin to see myself as this disgusting, obese creature, and I hated everything about me. I would stand in front of the mirror and degrade every portion of my body, head to toe.

I don't really know how it started, but I began throwing up my food. At first, I had to gag myself, but after a few times I could just throw up because I wanted to. As gross and pathetic as it is, it felt so good. It quickly becomes an addiction. It got to where it was never enough, and I would throw up every meal. Then sometimes I would eat a snack so I could make another deposit. I was scaring myself.

I asked my pastor for prayer. I made him promise that if I told him something, he would just pray and not lecture me. He promised, and he kept his promise. Then, because he was a man of his word, the enemy came in again trying to convince me that he did not care. At this point I felt like he was about the only one I could talk to. I didn't want my family to know what I was doing, so I wasn't going to talk to them. I do have a really good friend that I can talk to about anything, but I just couldn't make myself tell her yet. Her prayer usually comes with lectures despite her word, because she doesn't care about what I want as much as she cares about what I need.

I was serious when I asked for prayer, I wanted help. I stopped vomiting my food but every time I ate I could hear this voice yelling at me. "Do it! It feels good!" It really did feel good except on the days that I was to hoarse to talk or my ribs were aching from all the action. I picked the habit back up. I knew this was a bad idea but didn't not really care.

Satan's plan almost worked, and I began to entertain the thought that even my pastor did not care, but my pastor proved Satan wrong. He loved me through my entire battle. I can assure you I was not acting like a loveable saint. I continued testing the waters of sin, but it wasn't because I wanted to do these things; it was because I had all these voices screaming in my head! I needed to shut them up!

One day I remember texting Psalm 68:6 to my Pastor, the last part says, "but the rebellious live in a sun-scorched land." I told him my soul got sun burned. This landed me back in the office for more counseling and prayer. That was an interesting day. I really wanted my pastor's help but every time he would oblige, I would get so mad at him. He knew I was capable of more than I let on, so sometimes he would point me in the right direction and make me do the work and figure things out on my own. This was one of those days. Now, I'm thankful for leadership and not dictatorship, but then, I wanted him to be blunt and to the point. I understand now that his way led to growth. At that moment I didn't care about growth, I was just trying to survive.

During this trial, I tried alcohol a few times. My first attempt was that day. I still have texts messages between me and Pastor Chad, so I am going to share some of our dialogue with you.

Me: I am not tangled up in any particular sin right now, but I feel cold, removed, and my heart is hard. I don't think I am feeling conviction and I think that is what is scaring me. I was driving through the Blackwell/Morrilton area (closest wet county). The thought hit me that I could stop and get a drink… not enough to get drunk, just enough to see if I could feel convicted. I didn't do it, but I almost did. What stopped me is that I realized that I wouldn't be any better than (insert name of my friend who relapsed in previous chapter); a dog returning to his own vomit. That upset me, and I text someone while I was driving. I swerved in front of a semi. Then I got really upset. What if I died? Is that a risk I can take? No!

I went on to explain some random thoughts that raced through my head, but my conversation continued like this:

Me: *"I don't know what is wrong with me or how I got here, and I'm scared that I do not have time to figure it out on my own!"*

Pastor: *"That is great news! You are almost there! No time to figure it out by works (on your own). Grace is the answer! Grace is they way. Grace is the solution. Give it all up by grace and faith. Then submit to the layer peeling by the Holy Spirit! This is what revival is all about! Reviving us to a place of life!"*

My pastor really is a man of wisdom, but can I be honest and tell you this answer infuriated me? I felt like he only heard the good in what I had to say. He wasn't hearing the cry for help. He ignored the "I almost…" and skipped straight to the "but I didn't." Please understand how warped my mind was at this time. Satan was working overtime. "I told you he didn't care." Well, if pastor didn't care then I wasn't going to care. I even attempted to address it.

Me: *"You see great news, but I am sitting here trying not to bawl my eyes out. We are obviously looking at the same thing from opposite sides of the fence."*

Pastor: *"I know we are, but you are on the cusp of the greatest spiritual breakthrough of your life! Keep it up!!!"*

Did he say keep it up? I felt like he was congratulating me. For what, being a failure? I can keep that up! I stopped and got the drink and drank it all the way to church. Not much to tell except that I was right. I was not feeling conviction which only made my mind and heart worse.

My pastor tried to help me but at this point I could argue with a fence post. Although I really knew his heart was probably grieved for my soul, I continued to act as though I believed he didn't care. I feel like I was mean to him during most of this and I apologized to him repeatedly, but he was so gentle with me through it all. I told him about my drink. It was just one, but my church doesn't believe in drinking and no matter what, I am an honest person.

Pastor: *War is won one battle at a time. Battles are won one skirmish at a time. A skirmish is won by killing what stands in front of you now. Stop worrying so much about the war, just overcome the enemy in your face at the moment.*

This text gave me hope. It was kind of a breath of fresh air. This was when I was struggling with my kidney stone which consisted of a lot of complications. My husband, who knew nothing of the battle I was facing, offered to buy me alcohol to dissolve my kidney stones. At first, I resisted, but finally I gave in. In the eyes of my family, it was justified for medical reasons, but I knew the intent of my heart. I had every intention to get drunk. I had just begun my endeavor and God used my Associate Pastor to reach out to me. At this point she also knew nothing of the internal battle I was facing. This situation got ugly, so I will spare you the details. I found out quickly, that when God delivered me from alcohol, He did it right. I'm certainly not an alcoholic anymore!

One night, I even took a handful of pills. I was careful not to take too many, but I needed to get high enough to drown the rage out. Epic fail! Nothing I tried seemed to help; not the bad stuff or even prayer. I cried out to God nightly, but only with my words, not my heart. I ended up doing some counseling with both my pastors. Somehow, I ended up in such a deep depression. I wasn't sure if I wanted to live or die; all I knew was if I was going to live, then I wanted to live right!

I felt so hopeless and so empty, but I've read the story of Job and how God restored everything the enemy had stolen from him. I had read the story of the prodigal son, and how he was welcomed home with love. I had read story after story, but I found myself standing once again at the crossroad of grace. I could clearly see the path that I was supposed to take, but I couldn't convince myself that I was worthy.

If you find yourself in a pit where you are depressed, oppressed, fighting addiction or even suicidal, then please check out this sermon from my pastor.

- *Diseases of Despair*

The Wilderness

Have you ever read the book of Exodus? The Israelites were being held captive by Pharaoh. God sent Moses to Egypt. Moses was to insist on them being released. Moses had a spoken word from God, but it required obedience to bring forth results. Did Moses see results immediately? No, he did not. Pharaoh did not grant freedom to the Israelites until after God sent ten separate plaques.

Moses had obeyed. He did his part. He was not responsible for Pharaoh's actions, he was only responsible for his own obedience and reactions. If Moses would have not obeyed, or if he reacted out of impatience, then the fate of the Israelites could have been compromised.

Freedom at last... but did the Israelites find their promised land instantly? Again, the answer is no.

An eleven-day journey turned into a forty-year quest. How? Why? Mindset was a big factor. The Israelites had a negative mindset. Though God fed, clothed and protected them, they were ungrateful, fearful, whiny, and idolatrous. The shortest distance between two points is a straight line. Because the Israelites complained and grumbled, their journey had a lot of unnecessary twists and turns.

Sound familiar? I know I can identify with them. God gave me a promise; a spoken word. If I was obedient and acted according to faith, my journey to the promise could have been a straight shot. However, I listened to voices of reason and doubt. I hesitated! I let fear add bumps to my journey that could have been avoided.

I am the Moses in my story and Sarah is the Israelite that is being held captive. Through obedience and submission of my flesh, Sarah will be led to the that which God has declared over my life. There is a Pharaoh standing between Sarah and God's will. Who is it? My mind! My mind has a firm grip on Sarah. Sarah has tasted the manna of God, yet she often feasts on the comfort offered by the hand of Pharaoh.

The word wilderness translates from the Hebrew word midbar. When you chase the meaning to its original roots, wilderness means "a place of voices." It would make sense that my mind would be my biggest setback. However, the wilderness does not have to be a negative place. Even Jesus was led to the wilderness to be tempted, but He passed the test. Depending on my mindset, the wilderness can be a place of failure or a place of growth.

There is a place of milk and honey for me. How do I find it? How do I get there when I mess up more than I succeed? How do I keep sight of the straight line between Melissa and

Sarah, or Sarah and God when my mind is an overgrown wasteland? How do I arrive at my promise when I seem to fall so short?

The answer is GRACE!

If you need help finding your way out of the wilderness of your mind my Pastor has a sermon that can help shed some light.

- *The Place of Voices*

A Cry for Help

It's May 2018. I just completed the hardest one-year span of my life. It was May 2017 when we found out that my mom had cancer, and February 2018 when she graduated into eternal life. Losing my mom was hard. I don't want to dilute the hardship that I or my family endured, but at the same time, I have a peace knowing that my mom is in Heaven. She's healed and resting in a peace that we all long for. Though I miss her immensely, I wouldn't call her back to us if I could.

As hard as that battle was, my current battle was a lot harder. I can't begin to describe the torment that was going on in my head. Honestly, I didn't know if I would be okay. I knew all the things that God's word has declared over my life. I had a knowledge and understanding that He could forgive me and wipe my slate clean.

Psalm 103:10-12
He has not dealt with us according to our sins, nor punished us according to our iniquities. For as the heavens are high above the Earth, so great is his mercy towards those who fear Him; as far as the East is from the West, so far has he removed our transgressions from us.

If "head knowledge" had been enough, then I would have been fine. I fully understood what this passage meant; though I deserve to be punished, God chooses to forgive and forget- so why didn't He? Why was I still stuck in this pit of condemnation? The missing link was application. I must apply God's word to my life in order for it to be activated!

Matthew 6:14
For if you forgive other people when they sin against you, your heavenly father will also forgive you.

Mark 11:26
"but if you do not forgive, neither will your father who is in heaven forgive your transgressions."

Unforgiveness blocks God's forgiveness! So, who have I not forgiven? I've mentioned a few different situations in which I felt wronged by people, but I honestly felt like I had forgiven each of them. Was I really harboring unforgiveness? Yes, I was! I had to learn to forgive ME! It was easy to forgive those other people. Most of them didn't realize what they were doing, but this was different. I was harming myself. I was doing it deliberately, not caring what consequences I must face. This had to come to an end. After many calls, texts, and sessions with both of my pastors, and after confiding in one of my closest friends, I knew what I had to do.

One Saturday, my husband and daughter were both working. I drove to my church. I knew I could pray anywhere, but I wanted to get alone with God and avoid distractions. After arriving, I sat in my car for about thirty minutes before I convinced myself to go in. I had a little bit of office work that needed to be caught up. I did that first to avoid the real reason I was there.

My pastor knew I was there, and he knew even though I wanted to submit, I was struggling. He sent me a link to a sermon about grace. I sat in my office and watch the whole sermon, but still I felt nothing short of defeat. I text my pastor back saying, "I still can't make myself believe that I deserve Grace. Maybe, I should try to scare myself and convince myself that I don't deserve hell".

He responded back with another link for me to watch. This link was not a sermon. It was an artist telling her story about hell. God had given her a vision of hell, and then instructed her to paint what she saw. She described torment after torment in great detail. Any normal person would have cried out to God before the video ended. Not this calloused heart! I sat there for about two hours watching video after video on hell, trying to scare myself into repentance.

Nothing! I felt nothing! My pastor always tells us that faith has no feelings. I know that we are saved by faith, but I wanted to feel something...ANYTHING!

Ephesians 2:8
For it is by Grace you have been saved, through faith- and this is not from yourselves, it is the gift of God

I've received other gifts in the past that I did not feel worthy of receiving, but I didn't reject it, I simply accepted. So, I decided that's what I was going to do. It didn't matter if I "felt it" or not, I was going to submit my will and pray.

I got up from my desk, made the long walk to the altar, and sat down. I laid my head on the altar and that is as far as I got. I froze! For the next three hours I sat there, Indian style at the altar with my head down. Though I set there in complete silence, that was the loudest three hours of my life. Voices in my head were screaming- voices of failure, voices of defeat. They wouldn't shut up! I could hear Satan laughing at me as he mocked me. I had chills running all over my body. I don't mean the Holy Ghost goosebumps. Satan is real, and he was fighting hard to knock the last breath out of me. (Obviously, he didn't win, or I wouldn't be writing this book.)

1 John 4:4
But you belong to God, my dear children. You have already won a victory over those people, because the spirit who lives in you is greater than the spirit who lives in the world. (greater is He that is in me than He that is in the world)

After Five and a half hours total of fighting, I finally opened my mouth. *"God please forgive me! I want to live right. Please help me. Please close the mouth of the lion, just as you did for Daniel. Walk through this fire with me as you did for the three Hebrew children. God, I repent of all my wrong thoughts and actions. Help me to turn from these things."* My prayer was short, but that's all it took for God to step back onto the scene.

God loves us with compassion. What does that mean? We often translate the word compassion to love, which is correct, but God does everything in greater capacity than we do. Before God created us, He looked through time and saw that we would need a way of escape. He called that plan Jesus Christ, his only begotten son. His gut was wrenched, His heart torn open, and the most vulnerable parts of His being laid bare. This is compassion; this is the fierce love of God. Because God loves us to this capacity, He will leave the ninety-nine every time and come seek out the one. I was never able to comprehend the depth of that statement until recently when I lost my way and I became that one again.

I gained a new insight. God will go to any depth, any pit; He will combat any addiction or circumstance and He will recue His sheep at any cost. God does not care how mangled, bruised, or bloody we are- He loves us and will rescue us every time. God's love has no boundaries!

A Turn to Righteousness

Though I had repented of my wrong-doings, I was still fighting a battle that seemed bigger than me. To be honest, there were several times that I didn't believe I would come out on the winning side. I was consumed by condemnation. I knew that wasn't a God thing. I had the power to kick it to the curb, but I seemed to be a prisoner in my own mind!

The next morning, after repenting, I went to church. It was Mother's Day, but it was my day with God. I went to my home church that morning, then I went to my dad's church that night. God had orchestrated that whole day for me. I responded to the altar call, and I started an uphill climb. For the first time in a few months, I began to feel a possibility that I might be okay. Over the course of the next few weeks, I was all over the place. I was up and then I was down. I went to another counseling session with my pastors. It took a while, but we uncovered some roots. This is what they helped me learn:

First, I had roots of rebellion left in my life. Rebellion is more than outward acts of rebellion, it is a heart issue. The acts are the fruit that is bore after we allow the root to make a home in our heart. I honestly thought I had dealt with this, but there was a small fragment left. It only took a small, unnoticed fragment of rebellion to spin my mind out of control. A little leaven leavens the whole lump.

I was on a path of growth, and as part of my journey, God began to expose landmines that were hidden in my life. He began exposing them so that I could avoid them and call them out of my life through prayer. Instead, rebellion kicked in, and I smashed every landmine God had revealed causing explosion after explosion.

Secondly, He revealed that I was acting towards Him like a rebellious kid in need of attention.

God didn't fix my marriage. God didn't heal my sixteen-year-old daughter's health, who had asthma and Erbs-Palsy since birth. God didn't heal my mom, or so I thought at the time. It was official, God was ignoring me.

I have been stuck in the "can't hear Him, can't see Him, can't feel Him" stage for so long that out of desperation, I acted out in pure rebellion. One way or another, I was going to make God respond to me. God remained silent through my bad choices. I knew God was going to lash out at me in pure anger, but he didn't. I even expected my pastors to lash out, but they didn't either. I was shown love and grace through this entire battle. I kept pushing, and climbing, and seeking! My pastor kept texting and quoting the same scripture:

James 4:7
Submit yourselves, then, to God. Resist the devil, and he will flee from you.

I remember June 1st, 2018, while sitting in the Walmart parking lot, I was fighting the same thoughts in my head. I called my pastor. I was totally flustered. "What am I missing? What am I doing wrong?" I had submitted everything I need to submit. I had picked my Bible back up. I was praying, I was reading my devotions. The only thing that I could think of that I wasn't doing, was fasting. I believe in fasting, but remember, food was part of my battle. Fasting at this point would potentially be an extremely bad idea.

My pastor responded once again with that scripture. I remember interrupting him saying, "I have. It's not working." I don't play games with stuff like this. I was serious. Luckily, so was my pastor. He said "God's word never returns void. If it isn't working, then you are not submitting." "I am. I've submitted everything. Can you name one thing that I haven't laid down?" He responded, "I can tell you one thing. You haven't submitted your determination. You're still in flight mode. You have to buckle down and be determined that no matter what you face, no matter how hard, you will live for God."

I opened my mouth to argue, but then I quickly shut it. That resonated in me. That night, I couldn't sleep. I set up all night talking to God, reading His word, and watching sermons on YouTube. Around three in the morning, technically June 2nd, I felt prompted to write. That night was my bondage breaking moment. God spoke back to me. The voices in my head went silent. I've been great ever since and my joy has been restored. A few days later, God revealed and confirmed that my writing from that night, was actually chapter 1 of this book. I had that familiar "Sarah" moment where I question God. "Me? Write a book?" For about ten minutes I reminded God about how unqualified I am, but quickly I said, "Yes Lord." I'm so thankful I did.

Grace Defined

What is Grace?

<u>Grace</u> by definition is, the free and unmerited favor of God.

<u>Unmerited</u> means undeserved. I can not earn it nor can I buy it.

<u>Favor</u> means the approval, support, or liking of someone or something.

To Simplify this, grace means that God chose to love me, on purpose, just because He can! I don't have to earn or buy His love, I just need to accept it.

We've danced all around the subject of grace. Allow me to paint a picture of what grace looks like to me. Grace is the ability to come into the presence of God Almighty even though I am unworthy and undeserving. Grace is the fact that God will use me just as I am. Grace is the ability to realize the blood of Jesus Christ purifies me and makes me worthy. Grace is my adoption certificate that proves that I am his beloved daughter. Grace is my empowerment to live like Jesus. Grace is the essence of God infused in my heart. Grace overrides every label that the enemy tries to place on me. Grace is the "but" to all my failures!

"I was an alcoholic, but...."

"I was an addict, but..."

"I had a foul mouth, but..."

"I had a negative mindset, but..."

"I had a lack of faith, but..."

"I didn't feel worthy, but..."

+ I **G**ained **R**ighteousness **A**t **C**hrist's **E**xpense.

+ I am experiencing **G**rowing **R**evelation **A**nd **C**arnal **E**xecution.

+ I am **G**aining **R**est **A**fter **C**ondemnation **E**nded.

+ A **G**ap was **R**ealized **A**nd now I am **C**onnected **E**ntirely.

+ Now **G**od **R**eigns **A**nd **C**hrist is **E**xalted.

Grace is a door of opportunity that leads to Restoration.

What Does Restoration Look Like?

We are on different paths and we all face different battles. The curve balls life has thrown at me are going to be different than the ones you will be catching. Therefore, restoration will look different for you than it did for me.

For me, I got my joy back, no more depression, no more screaming rage and torment in my head. I have a genuine smile on my face and people are noticing the change. I'm talking to God daily. I can now pray freely in my heavenly prayer language.

More importantly He is talking back to me. God is making a beautiful message of grace and redemption out of the mess that I made. Though I had felt like I had no business working in my church, God expanded my territory. God has even been using me again to speak into other people. A good-paying job practically landed in my lap. I haven't really worked in years. I have no experience, but they handpicked me out of the stack of applications. My home needed repairs that we could not afford, but God made it happen and I didn't even ask. Then, God opened the door and currently we are in the middle of transition to Atkins, Ar. We will live a few minutes away from the church that I call home. God is just a good God that cares and knew what I had need of.

Remember, I had mentioned I was considering divorce, and God told me to wait on my promised Isaac? He didn't mean that I would meet a man named Isaac and fall in love. He meant that I would fall in love with David Brown, the man I had pledged myself to. I must be honest and tell you that I never thought it was possible. We were almost strangers who shared a home. I had resentment built up against him, but all that has been removed! He's not perfect. Neither am I, but over the last few months I've learned an important lesson about extending grace. Love is growing, and passion has been restored. I always said that I hate being touched. I really did. And in some ways, I still do. People are stunned when they see me walking hand-in-hand with my husband.

God is teaching me how to love and be loved; self-love is included. As Sarah blooms, God's light will be shown to a very dark world. I can already see so many areas where God has used me to make an impact. He used the best parts of me, and He used the worst. God created me. He knew I would make a total wreck of His plan, so He already had a GPS plan to reroute me. His plan will always prevail! I'm lucky to be a small part of it.

My chapter of restoration is still being written. Every day my life is a clean sheet of paper and my Master holds then pen. I am learning to allow Him to write freely. I trust Him and I know my story will end beautifully.

What's Your Name?

Hi, my name is Sarah. I'm just like you. I've been called out from sin, called out from this world, called out for a purpose. I am a daughter of the Most High King. I have potential. I have a promise. I am the head and not the tail, above and not beneath. I am more than a conqueror. I can do all things through Christ who gives me strength. I'm still learning who I am in Christ. Just like you, I'm learning to walk in obedience.

Who are you? Who do you see yourself as? Does it line up to who God says you are? My self-image did not match God's image of me. I never knew I could be anything other than Melissa, but God never gave up on Sarah.

I'm willing to bet that at some point when you read this book, you saw a glimpse of yourself. Our flesh and our spirit will always war against each other. The dog that you feed, is the dog that will win the fight. Even Paul struggled with this very concept.

Romans 7:15-20
I do not understand what I do. For what I want to do I do not do, but what I hate I do. And if I do what I do not want to do, I agree that the law is good. As it is, it is no longer I myself who do it, but it is sin living in me. For I know that good itself does not dwell in me, that is, in my sinful nature. For I have the desire to do what is good, but I cannot carry it out. For I do not do the good I want to do, but the evil I do not want to do—this I keep on doing. Now if I do what I do not want to do, it is no longer I who do it, but it is sin living in me that does it.

Look at the anointing on Paul's life. Look at how many lives were changed through his ministry. Paul faced struggles just like us. If God can restore Saul and use Paul, if God can restore Melissa and use Sarah, then what do you think he could do with your life?

**Isaiah 62:2
The nations will see your righteousness, and all kings your glory; And you will be called by a new name Which the mouth of the LORD will designate.**

God is calling you out of the boat of comfort. He has a new level for you. I don't know if you are unsaved, unchurched, or if you're a pastor of a mega church. It doesn't matter. There's always another level. God wants to give you a new name. Does this mean someone will come to you with the word of knowledge like they did me? Maybe not. It doesn't happen like that for everyone, but God is calling you by name; not the name that you see yourself as but the name that he destined you to be!

You were called for a purpose. You were created to be an asset to the kingdom of God. Satan has a plot to exploit you, but God has a plan to esteem you. God's plan may not make sense to you. I didn't understand where God was leading me, or why he chose me. I still can't believe I'm sitting here writing this book, but I trust God's plan for my life and I trust God's plan for yours.

As I revisited my journal, I learned things about myself. I realized things that God had been trying to show me all along, but I never saw before. It was like my life was a puzzle, and I had a lot of missing pieces. I'm a little more complete after this whole process. I highly recommend journaling about your life. I choose to write about the good and the bad; not so I can hold myself under condemnation, but so that I can remind myself of how far I've come! When Satan questions, "Where is your God?", I can pull out my writings and say "God was here all along. He never left me."

Though I couldn't see it, I now realize God really did carry me through the darkest time of my life. He is my comforter, my strength, and my best friend. I am victorious! You are victorious!

Seek God. Praise God. Pursue God. Abandon your will and trust His. When you feel that longing in your heart that is yearning for more of God, that's really Abba allowing you to feel His heart for you. That's right, Abba Father yearns after you.

Just as you are, not for who you will be someday!

"Becoming Sarah"

The journey of becoming Sarah
Was not an easy task,
It required much more of me
Than I thought God would ever ask.
I had to be submissive-
Not my will but His,
I had to overcome my fears
And be receptive to His gifts.
I had to let God tear down walls
That took me years to build,
I had to accept who I am through Christ
And allow my spirit to be filled.
I struggled with condemnation
And I didn't know my worth,
Satan had my mind warped,
Even after my second birth.
For years and years, I've struggled
And strived to run this race,
But one day at the altar
I caught a glimpse of Grace.
The concept of unmerited favor
Was a concept I couldn't grasp,
But one day God got ahold of me
Because one day I finally asked.
Since that day my life's been different,
I know longer feel the same-
So, one day as I was praying
I asked God to change my name.
God sent a word through Pastor
And I couldn't help but gasp.
My new name now is Sarah,
Our common trait is that we laughed.
God had given us both a promise
And for a moment we both had doubt
But I chose to guard this seed God planted
And see it "brought about".
He is the Potter and I am the clay
And I'm receptive to his molding.
For whatever reason God chose me
To be a vessel of His anointing.
So, Melissa will yield to Sarah
As Sarah yields to Christ
And I will walk in the promise you gave
Of an anointed, prophetic life!

NOTES

During the book, I made several references, with permission, to Pastor Chad Duvall's sermons. You can access these sermons by following our church on Facebook or YouTube.

www.facebook.com/abcaog/

www.youtube.com
Search Bell's Chapel Assembly of God

If you would like to reach me personally, please send an email to:

BecomingSarah2018@gmail.com

Dear Reader,

I bless you! I bless you with a heart to receive and ears to hear. I bless you with eyes to see the beauty God has placed within you. I bless you with the ability to accept God's call on your life. I bless you with hope and not despair. I bless you with peace and not chaos. I bless you with Grace and not condemnation. By the power of my words and by the authority of the Holy Spirit, I bless you with an abundant life in Christ Jesus.

Love in Christ,

Melissa Brown